About the Author

Victoria Day-Joel is the author of *Poetry Inspired by Oliver* (2018) and *New Beginnings* (2020). Awarded Love Reading's 'Indie Books We Love', she also writes articles on Vocal Media documenting life, loves, passions and the times we live in.

A Piece of Me

Victoria Day-Joel

A Piece of Me

Olympia Publishers
London

www.olympiapublishers.com
OLYMPIA PAPERBACK EDITION

Copyright © Victoria Day-Joel 2023

The right of Victoria Day-Joel to be identified as author of
this work has been asserted in accordance with sections 77 and 78 of
the Copyright, Designs and Patents Act 1988.

All Rights Reserved

No reproduction, copy or transmission of this publication
may be made without written permission.
No paragraph of this publication may be reproduced,
copied or transmitted save with the written permission of the publisher,
or in accordance with the provisions
of the Copyright Act 1956 (as amended).

Any person who commits any unauthorised act in relation to
this publication may be liable to criminal
prosecution and civil claims for damage.

A CIP catalogue record for this title is
available from the British Library.

ISBN: 978-1-80439-095-5

This is a work of fiction.
Names, characters, places and incidents originate from the writer's
imagination. Any resemblance to actual persons, living or dead, is
purely coincidental.

First Published in 2023

Olympia Publishers
Tallis House
2 Tallis Street
London
EC4Y 0AB

Printed in Great Britain

Dedication

To Big Nanny and Little Nanny

Acknowledgements

Dedicated to all my beautiful family and friends in celebration, to those who've shared these memories and been an inspiration.

Mum, Dad, Sarah, Dave, Chloe, Carla, Stanley Rhys, Alex, Joe, Eileen, Mark, Han, Emily, Charlotte, Glynis, Merv, John, Teresa, Jan, Nick, Lottie, Jasmine. The Day family, Enid, Ivan, Big Hair, The Bandit, Dave the Rave, Michelle, Thomas, Rob, Richard, Lyn, Steph, Mimi, Mr P, Cheyenne, Jo, Becky, Kristie, Judy, Sue M, Matt, Stu, Oliver, Samuel, Skid, Nikki, Elaine, James, Jason, Helen G, Rachel R, Simon, Jamie B, Jamie, Neil, Mark, Steve, Sylvia, Pat, Janet, Helen F, Mel, Carrieanne, Charlie, Cathalar, Sophie, Amy, Grant, Brian, Matthew, Sarah U, Julie, Terry, Salsa Mummy, Avisha, Sue C, Andrea, Jayne, Rob W.

Debs and Iona at The Braai House, Sarah & The Team at Havanas Coffee, John & Caroline at Cirencester Waterstones. Mash Guru, Darren Reddick at Planet Rock, Olympia Publishers and Vinit, my number one fan! Thanks for your support.

Introduction

Reading and writing come hand in hand: for the number of ideas whirling around my head to get down on paper, come a handful of books I can't wait to read all at once.

I'm a speed reader with an eclectic mix of books on the go. When reading biographies, I remember the wild and obscure stories that stirred the imagination, as if you're living the moment with that person, conjuring up imagery.

Remember the clothes you wore? The exact moment you heard that song played? The goose pimples on your body the first time you met that someone, thoughts or words etched in your mind through love, friendship, sadness.

I'm sharing poetry inspired by growing up in the 80s, teenager of the 90s, the social and cultural movements and life events that have shaped me, those stories that get re-told in times of reunion and the day-to-day.

We all have our own version of the same event told through different eyes, driven by the feelings and emotions held in that space in time; these are 'A Piece of Me'.

Feet

Small babe, long feet they say
Early school memories dipped in the paint
Picnics with Nan, barefoot on the kitchen floor
When it's too wet to walk in the grass, I can see the fields
from the window
Now and again, I trip and fall
Through clumsiness and mistakes
Let them take you where you desire
Learn from the footsteps, older doesn't mean wiser
Even if it's the wrong direction, it's the journey that counts
Believe a step forward is a step towards something greater.

Cambridge 1979: I was born 11 weeks premature
Astrologically, Mars was in my natal birth sign of
Aquarius.
Mars, 'The God of War', a planet of instinct and
survival.
Well, it turns out I like to fight against the odds.
My first three months were in an incubator fighting for
survival.
I was my parents' 'miracle baby'.
For the first time my father prayed and vowed if I
survived, he would pray every day.
To this day he still does.

Born in the 70s

Falling asleep listening to your favourite cassette
The one you played until it became loose and chewed-up brown tape
Rubik's cube, Roller Skates, Youth club
Bag of chips under £1
Penny sweets Blackjacks and Fruit Salad
Just seventeen, Kylie and Jason
Saved by the Bell, The Big Breakfast
Playing in the woods, riding miles on your bike
Reversing the charges from a red phone box
Dad, can you pick me up?
Embassy number 1, £1.21, holes in the cinema seats.

Some choices made are still true to heart today.
Others were fads or passing fancies.
Something new to learn to teach us everything is an experience to shape our future.
Growth is also unravelling layers of conditioning and understanding why we make the choices we make and why we made the choices we made.

Choices

Mankind have chosen for animals to suffer
Do they know their fate when packed in the crate?
I looked into sheep's eyes, cramped up, dead inside, scared
with fear and wide eyed
The life that they lead is to breed, not to succeed
Animals are sentient like you and me
Could you watch the way they are slaughtered?
When you eat meat at your leisure
Are animals really for eating pleasure?
Or to die in the name of sport or a cultural ride
Flogged and whipped with crushed insides
When life is exchanged for money
A needless greed, existence is a death sentence
No choice to breathe
We see the pretty end-package with garnish and flowers
Who sees the pain behind the blood and the feathers?
So have a think when you see the tusks, teeth and wear your
accessories of leather
The choices are yours but it takes a collective
To change and stand together.

Vegetarianism:
We cannot change the choices we have made
but we can make new choices for our future.

I first became vegetarian age eleven; I was very much interested in animal rights, anti-animal testing, anti-fox hunting, I would write to local MP Geoffrey Clifton Brown a pre-written template letter and wait eagerly for any replies.
My bedroom wall had a large Dolphins poster, my photo albums filled with cats and dogs.
As well as L'Enfant (the Man and baby Athena) poster iconic 80s image!
As a teenager, I started eating bacon and although I would mostly disguise the taste of meat from any unwanted thoughts about the animals, it was in my 30s I rescued a baby lamb from a country road to reunite with its mother and looked at it, thinking 'how can I ever eat meat again?' So from that day onward I didn't!

Growing Pains

Don't Doubt
To anyone unsure, it will be okay
You are stronger than you know
You are more beautiful than you see
To the girl sitting in her bedroom writing in her diary
You are good enough and perfect as you are
Don't waste time on those who dim your light
Love and believe you have everything you desire from within.

We all have insecurities and need reminders from time to time.
During adolescence and early adulthood, I was troubled with skin issues.
Looking in the mirror and wanting it to all disappear and just be like everyone else.
But 'everyone else' has their own issues too, they often feel bigger when they are in your own head.

Walking Past Memories

I pass the place when Nan once lived
Not knowing years later, I would become a neighbour
It looks warm and inviting as if you are still there
But those are the fond memories
Warmth still shines from your windows
As spirit never dies
Remembering the fun times
Fish and chips on Friday
Finding your hearing aid in the refrigerator
Jammy dodgers biscuits you called 'Dodgy Badgers'.

In memory of Nanny Kit.

First Time

The butchers and bakers were memory makers
Summer nights hanging out at 'the slide'
Leg in a cast, you caught my eye
In a small room we kissed without a lifeline
So nervous, you heard my heart beating
Some things you will always remember because they are the first times
And now the allotments and fields are filled with concrete
New houses with walls and boundaries
We felt free, like cats we roamed the streets
Nature was our playground viewed through young, sparkly green eyes.

And it was your name written on my school pencil case.

Menstrual

Emotions close to the surface
There is nothing wrong
It's just the first day of rain
Menstrual tears
Let them out, let them flow
Another day the sun will shine.

Hormones: driving life between storm rain and rainbows.

Morzine

A treat to a ski-resort as a hard-working team
In two's, the boss and bandit take to the skis
I'll try a snowboard, wearing a rainforest scene
Two sit and admire the snow-peaked view
Après is fondue and wine, followed by club time
luminous-green shot temptations take the night
With a pole, dancing, photographs with strangers
But we're sick and emotional and now we're drunk
And I can't pronounce the language to order a taxi ride home
We make it up the mountain
And up steep chalet stairs
Passing out fast without care
Our boss falls down the stairs
And pairs have to sleep on air
A lucid sleep until the next day
With peaky eyes and an aftertaste
Flights are cancelled, we have back-up by car
Squeezed amongst luggage and gifts of charcuterie
Wafting between the fresh mountain air
Altitude brings sickness as we make the long journey
A story to tell, how we made it home
In time for Christmas day and Mary announcing news of a baby who was to be a boy.

Estate Agents on tour 2006:
I joined an Estate Agents in 1997, my first full-time job as Office Administrator. It was only that I attended a CLAIT course to fill in my hours at college that I had some skill, which was typing with two fingers! (I still do that now, just a bit faster!) And a first-aid course which the boss joked I could help the mortgage advisor who was not feeling too well!

I was there eleven years, moving up the Agency ranks as negotiator & managing a new branch in Tetbury, Gloucestershire where you would occasionally see a glimpse of Prince Charles coming out of Highgrove.

Inappropriate Hours

I'm sat here wanting to message you
Not knowing what to say
Do I need an excuse or permission to ask if are you alone?
Do you even want to hear from me?
It's midnight! Why am I thinking these thoughts?
So many questions, do they even need asking?
Internal dilemma, you set my mind racing
Now I'm off to sleep
And you have no idea, how I want you over every inch of my body.

Lust and desire set your soul on fire.

Instinct

When attraction arrives
Like a thunderbolt
Unexpected, out of the blue
Your eyes, just alive
I realise I'm looking for longer
Uninterrupted
Admiring
Eyes naturally draw to your open shirt, with one too many buttons undone
You know how to look good
Yes, you know!
Chest hair exposed
I'm excited, are my eyes dilated?
Someone suddenly comes between us
What happened!
How can I remove the prey?
The strength of pleasure, that split-second thought
Attraction strikes, like cupid's bow
Here you are and gone too soon
Where did you come from?
Venus is where you belong.

The strength of the moment when meeting an attractive stranger.

Dreamscape

Now I ponder my dreams
Because I feel like I'm still in them
Examining how they came to be
As if I live a parallel life in the land of dreams
Daily events from a different lifetime
Or the same life but a different place
Or it's a person I know with a different face
Did I rest? Did I roam?
I guess some things you will never get to know
A hidden life called dreamscape, as if the day is the sun that casts the night-time shadow
Ready to be explored in the land when your head touches the pillow.

I often have a flash feeling the following day, from the dream I had the night before. How do we navigate the land of dreams?

Deep

Attracted by the deep blue sea
For a new life, just you and me
The journey began
A New Generation
Alive for the first time
One sip and I'm addicted to the devil
Music and Motorways
Visits with Champagne
But was I temptation that shouldn't have been?
Magnetic attraction and bedroom bliss
Masquerades a blue sky turned grey
Becoming a smokescreen for shattered dreams.

I wanted the fairy-tale
But it was escapism and blindness
Whilst skipping through a field of red flags
Of lessons yet to be realised.

Barcelona

Naked on the bed
Waiting for me
Like an unwrapped present
I can't wait to play with
Taking me by surprise
Pinching myself
Because you were mine.

A holiday memory – our first time away together, sometimes it's not the tourist sights you remember!

444

I was supposed to really feel
I was supposed to really see
Open Pandora's box
To know who I am and become the real me.

When the moth hit the flame,
Sometimes you meet someone who changes you, feelings like you have never felt or experienced before, someone who opens you up to every emotion and all its intensity, seduction, red-blooded allure, temptation and the curse of these depths of passion such as jealousy and paranoia. In the name of 'love' chasing the moments of euphoria, and going back for more, a self-perpetuating cycle, hard to break.

Toxic Heart

Our toxic heart of light and dark
Sparks fire burning from within
Suffocating our souls of sin
Ashes are those near and dear
Torn apart by pain and fear
A rose that grew chained us two
Spikes and vines of lovers entwined
Now bleeds our toxic heart.

If it were just the two of us in the world
Like Adam and Eve in our bedroom of Eden
We said it would have been forever.

Reflect

To the relationships before
That helped me grow
To the words that hurt
But made me know
Reflections showed your shadow
It was never my show
Feel the light within
When you find 'the one' you'll know.

We learn only when we are ready to learn.
Reflection provides space to learn and grow.

Dolly

I ask myself, If I fall out of love with you every weekend
How can you be any good for me?

Working nine till five, what a way to make a living?

Southern Girl

I crossed the north-south divide
To a land that spoke of Ginnels and Barm cakes
'Ey up' 'my chuck' 'my duck'
Northern boys love chips and gravy
The weather is damp across this industrial landscape
The land is rugged and ever changing
Even the clouds are less fluffy over the peaks
I see reservoirs, lakes, train tracks and canals
Two up, two down red-brick terrace with matching chimney stacks
This Gloucestershire girl settled well into cobbled streets.

2010-2016 I made Greater Manchester my stomping ground.
A new set of work friends made me feel I had a family away from home, moving away for the first time.
Estate Agency always had a new daily drama to keep you occupied; I had a partner in crime, we started working together on the same day; I had the agency knowledge, he knew the area, so it was a formidable team.
In the first week, we pranged the new sign written car, as I piled it high with Valentine's balloons to take home to my boyfriend.

One day we were out on a valuation together and a gust of wind lifted my skirt in a Marilyn Monroe moment and a toot came from a lorry driving past. We just laughed and laughed.

Away from the work walls I took up Salsa dancing, forming a fun group and meeting new people.

Healing Crystals

Ancient magic in a tumble stone
Untapped power within
Universal energy is a master to all
But do we know?
Mankind can receive it, if we just believe it
Purity, white, a stream of light
Engulf your spirit
Like a Body of water
Your path to wisdom and power
Is within.

A visit back home and day trip to Stroud for lunch with my mum and partner led to an unexpected and re-ignited passion.
I had always been an 'impulse buy' shopper and we finished the day in a shopping precinct café for coffee and cake; a beautiful carved wooden wizard staff caught my eye with a crystal ball on top.
It was expensive, it was gorgeous but I put it back thinking 'I can't buy another random object just because I like the look of it.'
It would sit in a cupboard somewhere, like the bright pink electric cheese grater I never used!
So we made our way back to the car park and I just

stopped and said wait! I've got to go back and 'buy it', it really was a calling. The lady behind the counter said, you need to cleanse the crystal. And this was the work of the crazy wood man.

I had no idea how to cleanse a crystal, but I felt I had to do it justice and wanted to look after my new purchase and was quite intrigued, even about the crazy wood man and where might I find him?

I read, you can cleanse crystals in spring water, a natural water source. My parents lived next to a river so off I went the same day down to the stream, bathing my new crystal in the water, still not knowing if I was doing this properly.

As I walked back, the neighbours caught sight and probably wondered what is that girl doing coming from the river with a wizard staff, but I didn't much mind!

After this I had a passion to learn about the healing power of crystals and found a spiritual teacher which was the start of healing myself and my spiritual journey in becoming a holistic therapist.

And knowing what I know now, the crystal was programmed and this was my calling.

My first crystal in my collection when I was a child was an Amethyst and so I became Amethyst Healing!

My Trusted Friend

To whom I danced with
shared glitz and glamour
We helped each other cross
Colloquial boundaries
Without knowing where we were heading
A new path appeared.

In 2016, I unexpectedly moved back to the Cotswolds as I was seeking a Monday to Friday job and no opportunities presented themselves locally.
I was looking for a role that would allow me to switch off from at the end of the day and allow me to develop my therapy business in the evenings and weekends, nurturing my passion for healing.
Little did I know this position would take me on a new journey; I was about to work with and meet my muse, propelling me in a new direction to open myself up and write my story.

Friday

Out we go dressed up for the show
Mistaken seats, we drink to the beat
Before we know it takes a psychedelic tone
Tequila downed and an angry man sounds
We walk the car parks for the lost and found
But it's all in our stride, because were out for the ride
Amaretto fuels the early hours, warming the way with cards and the sound of guitar.
Morning comes waking up to a strum, I sing along, this is nicer than birdsong
We communicate to learn and grow, it's this which feed and water our soul
My beautiful friend I love your company, when it's time to go we share a hug for the road.

We're two of a kind, our connection is healing, our friendship has meaning.
Whatever opens these deep feelings is bringing a lifetime of light through our souls.

Reincarnate

Maybe we are just
Star-crossed lovers
Past life re-enactors
Timeline jumpers
From Atlantis to Lemuria
Across the Pyramids
To this modern day
I'll bury my hidden treasure
For you and my ancestors
to visit incarnate someday.

Do you believe you've previously walked this earth or felt a person so familiar it's as if you had met them before?

Pollution

Pollution is gossip
Pollution is greed
Spreading like a smog
That covers the beauty

Pollution is the mind that is conditioned
Unexplored, nor open
That prevents us from
Trusting and believing

Pollution is ego
That prevents us from helping
From asking, for caring

Pollution is advertising
Feeding insecurities
Believing you cannot live without
Offering promise that leads
to debt and a shallow existence

Pollution is pressure
To keep up with your neighbours

Pollution is addiction to social media
To portray only your best side

It's already taken you to the dark side

When a photo is more important
than enjoying the moment
If you can't hold a conversation
Without looking at your phone

Then head for the trees
As nature is beautiful
A walk to clear your thoughts is free.

Removing our own personal 'poison' is having an awareness of what that 'poison' is and working on it to take ownership of ourselves.
We all have the power within to make changes and so too are we responsible for giving it away.

Out for a Ride

A drive to the cash point machine
I noticed the family cat on top of my mini
But half distracted and chatting away
Ignition was on, speed up, change gear
Then a neighbour points in dismay
Oh no! Things are not okay
This cat is still on the roof and out for a joy ride
I hear a scratch above as nails cling to the soft top
Quick, Emergency stop!
Looking through the rear-view mirror
To my cat with nine lives run off!

**Tabitha cat was safe and well after the incident.
I've not driven with a cat on the roof of my car since.
Just a plate I forgot to remove once which came on a 2-mile trip!**

Talking Fruit

I wonder if people say "that's that author
walking down the road with a pineapple in her hand"
And it brings back memories when I chased Laurence
Llewellyn Bowen
for a signature of his book, through the streets of
Cirencester
Me shouting "I've got a" to him, finish the sentence with "a
lovely bunch of coconuts"
And so, the circle turns and now I'm an author of a book in
Cirencester, but who is chasing me down the street?

Inspired by a conversation with Brian walking down a street in Cirencester.

Revolving

When one door opens, another is left behind
Your old is another's persons new
Once cherished and loved could become the loathed or lost
A parking space, clothes taken to charity, a job!
So do not fear what you no longer have space for
As someone else will be wanting to embrace their new and your old
The revolving door of Life.

Often we have to let things go to be ready to embrace the new.

Midlife Crisis

Is a 'midlife crisis' society's label?
Given to someone who's not afraid to live by unconventional rules?
Perhaps they are an awakened soul with spiritual clarity
Doing something a little different?
Can lead to judgement by the norm
Maybe 'mid-life' is an age where you know yourself
You know what you want and you don't care what someone thinks about it!

A friend once told me, "Someone will have something to say whatever you do, no matter what age you are." So, the moral of the story is: Fear not, if it feels right, then do it for yourself, you are worth it. And if something makes you happy, then it is well worth it.

Pieces of Paper

Going through my life in papers
Coming across the old and new
Hopes and dreams
Big events, some unforeseen
Wishes well of documented milestones
Yoga and afternoon tea never redeemed
Mindfulness and life coaching papers took a backseat
Now the plans are for overseas, a new dream
It could be your mistakes that are documented in history somewhere
Only the achievements hang on the wall
If you don't marry or raise a family
You won't grow another branch on the family tree.

Find your soul tribe
Grow your own branches through love and connection
It doesn't need to be recorded on a piece of paper
You can always send love by putting pen to paper.

Growth

You're making me move on without you
Encouraging me that I don't need you
You've held my hand
Is it time to let go?
And as I think, the salty tears burn my eyes red
Streaming, about to overflow
And you are calm and still
As what is meant for you is meant to be
Which way is the tide turning?
I'm crying because I'm coming to terms
With what I know to be right
The wind is howling for me
The rain is pouring with me
I have to let go and let you be
And I wonder, where I had kept my tears hidden?
As they burst from the seams undoing lock and key
Emotions getting the better of me
Rising so high they can only seep out as tears.

A different shade of melancholy today
Expectations with you have faded away.

Time

I'll forget the feelings that were a struggle
It's easy to, once they've passed
Slowly a grey hair appears
Slowly a wrinkle appears
Slowly your body adapts
Cells renew every day and then you realise 'I've changed.'

Becoming a woman, you realise that insecurities are just a part of yourself that you need to accept.
We can forgive ourselves at any time and start a new mindset any day we choose.
Remember to 'self-talk positively' to yourself with love and respect each day and you will only accept the same from others.

My Body

Let thoughts speak to me kindly
My mouth savour the fuel that feeds me
My eyes appreciate beauty
This is my body
A gift
A vessel to move earthly.

When the physical, emotional, mental and spiritual are in unity.

Seeking Asylum

Your words are more powerful when I can hear your voice
I can't imagine having to run from all that I know
Pain and fear, from the ones who say they love you
The ones who are blood, should be looking after you
Yet, fill you with terror and expose you to violence
When homelessness can feel like refuge because you fled war
A temporary relief, the battle continues
It's a new culture, a new beginning
You feel like an outcast because of the colour of your skin
All you want to be is accepted
You cry because you can't speak the language
Can you trust officials to help you? Can the government make you legal?
Still the past carries with you and new people don't understand you
Please find comfort with the kind souls who have helped you.

'Where there is light' was an exhibition by the charity GARAS at Gloucester Cathedral.
Supporting refugees and asylum seekers in Gloucestershire
A powerful moving display from refugees from Sudan, Iran, Syria and Pakistan.

Awake

I can't stand to see hurt or suffering
It's not for others to fix
It's for us to see and make a change
Homeless are not invisible
Bullying is not acceptable
Nobody is invincible.

For the love of our planet and humanity, remember compassion and kindness.

February

Roadkill frozen at the side of the road
Preserving death from the day before
The frost softening macabre with a glisten
I can't be oblivious
This would have been their home
A road between a canopy of trees
We all need a safe highway
To live safe and harmoniously in nature.

In the Netherlands, USA and Canada, architects and conservationists have built wildlife bridges and tunnels to help animals safely cross the road; let us build more animal highways.

Pandemia

The virus came and it made us think
Lockdown, a sudden Stillness
We slowed down and wondered can we carry on?
With plans and dreams then fear creeps in

You still need to see the beauty
Without the natural world we would not be
This is the first in my lifetime
I see on a global scale we are all suffering

Only now from this western world
We understand we were privileged
The daily reality for billions
Life for all has become about health and survival

Behind my door, there is no make-up
I've become a little messy, my body's hairy
The world outside has become scary
And now I know the rules, I won't turn on the TV

I'm a little bit low on the day the rain came
I can't visit you for escape and emotional security
To see your face and bright eyes
I'm becoming my own comfort blanket

I realised I do have self-sufficiency
And enjoy peace and tranquillity
The pressure is off, there is no race
Life was moving ever so quickly.

March 2020: 'Lockdown'. A poignant time in history, the roads became bare, and an eerie stillness filled the air. Who notices when life is a green light? When things are running smoothly, you think it will be that way forever. As soon as the light turns red, you stop and notice you can't move anywhere.

Adjustment

At my worst I'm looking at human contact as if humans have turned into vampires
Visualising garlic and a cross around my neck with a sprinkle of protective herbs and crystals for good measure just to go out grocery shopping
At my best I'm romanticising a sunny day where I can meet my love
We would sit in a lush green field in the sun for a two-metre picnic
The desire for a kiss, to see your eyes, even a peep through a window
It really is your whole being that I miss, my lover
And my four-legged friend who doesn't understand why I've not been to visit.

Lockdown was lone time, floating like driftwood, not knowing where you would end up.

Heavier

This coat feels heavier in winter
Wrapping up my emotions with
A layer of I miss you
A layer of sadness
A longer day of darkness
Succumbing to another sugar craving
To beat the blues of Covid away.

Winter 2020.

Balance

Visualise a clear road free from obstacles
Some days it will be long and bumpy or dark and shadowy
Sometimes the weeds will hide the flowers
But when the blue sky breaks it brings an epiphany
Keep the path of light in your heart.

Ups, downs are inevitable, as long as you believe in the light, it will return. We all have days where emotions can bring us down.
I'm not carrying my baggage; I just view it as it goes past on the conveyor belt called 'life!'

The Year of the Hermit

Lockdown has opened up a love of being a hermit from home
You can watch live feeds without being seen
Not have to do your hair or make-up or even wear clothes
You can dip in and out, just observe or engage
And still feel part of a community
It's my type of freedom being a hermit from home
Open up the transmitters or batten down the hatches
Naked dance, who would know?
And what did you find in the cupboards?
Well, I have a new hobby. Yes! I have been baking scones
And I questioned whether a twenty-four pack of toilet rolls was acceptable to buy
When it was the only one left on the shelves!

As each day passes, the pandemic starts to become the norm and finding simplicity can be most joyous, sometimes you forget the pleasures.

Uncensored

Some nights I want your head between my legs
To feel the desire, ignite in our eyes
Electrical bursts of a lover's bite
Taken over by animalistic senses
The smell of your skin
Longing for play to begin.

Sometimes all you want are pleasures of your lover.

Summer

A comfort blanket that bathes me in silk and petals that smell of orange blossom
A renewed joy to life, buzzy, nutty, smell of sun lotion reminds me of holidays
I'm light, airy, dancing with grace
Moving like the spirit of a horse run free.

And here begins my favourite season.

Nude

Intimacy plays as flashback vision
A lover's touch feels best
After our clothes have fallen to the floor
Skin on skin, no line between
The ultimate sacred act
Fullness of the senses
Passion eyes
Raw and wild
To ask for what you desire
The word 'deeper' penetrates harder
Memories linger longer
Forever in an afterglow with you.

Covid Bubbles:
I cried the first time we could open our doors and be able to kiss and touch each other again.
All at the same time feeling vulnerable, were we safe?
And if we were, I feel conflicted as there are many others who are unsafe in the world.

In My World

We would take time to meditate daily
Learn how to sew, make and mend clothes
Grow plants, herbs and vegetables
Learn their medicinal benefits
Try a new skill each month to see if we had a natural ability
Speak to spread encouragement and ideas
Express feelings without judgement
Walk barefoot in the summer sun
Embrace all cultures through loving arms
Dance, sing, be your favourite weirdo
Teach self-care to enhance self-worth
Encourage independence
Know we are capable of healing ourselves
Share and care for animals, nature, to be at one.

I'm living life as my authentic self, as the seasons change, I'm becoming free.
Giving away my belongings ready to move on. Maybe I can visit them again in friends' and family's homes like a museum but more likely it will look like a bric-a-brac store!

October

Integrating autumn, anticipating winter
It feels like a time of cinnamon and spice
Warming chocolate and ginger
To move these cold bones
A pocket of September Sun
Feeling so precious
Yet sadness as we say goodbye
Like a farewell from your lover
When you won't see them for some time
The sun is my heart, it's fading away
Integrating autumn, anticipating winter.

Beauty comes with change, because you see through fresh eyes.
A piece of my heart is always left in Summer.

Missing

You're the glisten through the trees across the icy ground
I need you to feel alive
wrapped in layers just to feel a passing glance
Warmth embraces, you move higher
The seasons are nature's way of reminding us
We are forever changing and so will the way I feel you.

I feel low as the light fades, on the grey days
Through the depths of winter when you've gone away.

Shady Wood

If only for today, I would live at a cabin in the woods
Amongst the birdsong and trees as a canopy to climb, to see the view from a Raven's eye
Shady moss banks, stone walls and hidden nooks to explore creatures in their castle
Snails and earthworms as the groundsmen
Sinking my soles into the earth
Mud trails leading back to warm lights
A blanket in front of an open log fire with that smoky smell which lingers on the skin
A mug of cocoa and a rosy glow into the nightly hours.

I've discovered a new walk, a hidden gem that feels home from home to which the landscape and nature are inspiring and this escapism isn't hurting anyone!

The Empath

I don't know you but I feel you
It's always been a sense through energy
I just didn't realise until now
Communicating with your energy not your words
So, excuse me if I respond a little strange
I'm computing what I've heard after I've felt you.

Empaths have big hearts and sensitive souls.

Mid-Air

My spark has dimmed
I've lost my mojo
I'm in limbo, no man's land
On a bridge between my old life and the new one I've created.
It's here but not ready yet, so where do I live?
In a flat with just a bed or a van that doesn't move with my belongings
In the middle of nothing I can see
With a whirlwind or thoughts inside of me
Sometimes you have to trust the Universe will deliver and hang in mid-air.

When the life you visualised isn't ready yet!

Goodbye

I looked at your grandeur knowing it would be the last time
You've kept me safe and warm
But it wasn't always that way
When I felt confined and needed an escape
Connection to spirit brought peace and calm here
Cherubs and angels are part of your history
A sanctuary and retreat
Emotions held between these stone walls.

After thirteen years of ownership, I've finally packed my bags, turned the key in the lock for the last time and now I can make my way to a new life, heading to the sun.

Cycles

My energy is waning like the moon
But l will rest, replenish and come back more exuberant
Listen to her cycles
Love La Luna
La Luna, La Luna.

The moon is small, pretty and delicate but behind the facade she is big, strong and powerful despite all you can see.

To embrace the phases, I check my diary with the lunar cycle.
New Moon is a time to rest and replenish.

Universal Message of Love

Love is the magical seed of growth
Atoms and molecules fusing
An internal firework of celebration
Vibrations
Like wind chimes across the warm breeze
Soothing balmy
Love is understanding
It's nurture breeds
Encouragement waters independence
Smile, touch, gaze
Breathe the essence
of eternal existence
As the sun returns
Physical becomes spiritual
Spiritual becomes physical
Through the gateway of womankind
A newborn from the womb of water still has to learn to swim
Sow seeds to pollinate and dance in the wind
Be a hand that lifts the earth
A mind that raises the universe
Through the universal message that is love.

Celebrating the mid-summer sun, re-birth and the

beauty of nature.
Variety is the spice of life.
As I lay in the sun, where do I place my mind?
In the book I just read.
Because now it's time to have some fun and move on.

Romance

Hold me in the moment
Of a glint so magnetising
A kiss so sensual, I want you everlasting
Where each touch is waiting for the next
Explore me as the most beautiful map of the world
As senses explode into lustful oblivion
Desire will replay this over and over
So a moment with you can last forever.

To keep the excitement of first romance is to hold your loved one in your heart when apart
In flashback memories, through a message to show they are in thought is daily care.
The build-up of excitement in anticipation, creating that spark of newness yet as if you've never been apart.

Blaze

In an instant you intoxicate my air
with summer sweetness
The high is alive
as footsteps are the only sound to exist
Senses on the breeze
Tasting the cream of chocolate
Blossoms moving like confetti
Riding the baseline
Lost in the music
I want coffee stronger
Music louder
T O U C H M E
F E E L ME
I want to be taken harder
As all my
S E N S E S F I L L
I want more
C O M E W I T H M E into summer wildness.

Flow through me in waves of forgotten time.

Wildness

Shower me in confetti
of wild romance
As verdant as the land love roams
Majestic as first light on
a white stallion
As fertile as summers sown
Vivid in the way we grip bodies
Unable to let go.

Let passion run through you like a wildfire in the wind.

Explore

Chemicals engulf our blood stream
As we explore carnal sweetness
Through a long sensual line
Arms high lengthening the torso
To lips welcoming you in a velvet glove
Moaning as you grow harder
Push and pull of hair across face
Writhing back and forth
Pleasure soars as hands are pinned into submission
Your gaze passes the jewel of my breast
Down a tattooed naval
Eyes lead hand to the place of desire
Rocking and pressing to the ultimate high
To feel satisfied is to feel your bodily fluid inside me
To wear our scent and taste as a coat of arms
Wrapped around our bodies long after sweet pleasure.

You've fed me with desire
until we meet again
Entering me has given new oxygen
Don't leave me too long
Without a drip feed to your nectar.

A Piece of Me

A piece of me is unwrapped with you
Softness is reciprocated with nurture and care
Your kiss is a wish to become everlasting on my lips
Life is full of joy, exuberance and wonder
Exploring unknown nomadically
Freedom excites
For what is yet to come is imagination unleashed
You're the sweetest surprise
So loving and gentle
You've filled me with new warmth
I'll share with you everywhere
Abundance and beauty
Hold me in your heart as a piece of you.

When lost in your kiss
envelop me in your arms so I can't float away
I've discovered a new piece of me when I'm with you
The blessings you count now, hold the dreams to your future.